Classic
Quotations

Classic
Quotations

Memorable musings that put life in perspective

ARCTURUS

This edition published in 2014 by Arcturus Publishing Limited
26/27 Bickels Yard, 151–153 Bermondsey Street,
London SE1 3HA

ISBN: 978-1-78212-868-7
AD004031NT

Printed in China

Contents

Life's Journey 7

The Wide World 65

All You Need Is Love 129

The Art of Life 193

Success and Failure....................257

The Lighter Side of Life 321

It's never too late to have a happy childhood.

Tom Robbins

The beautiful thing about learning is that nobody can take it away from you.

B.B. King

I feel sure that
no girl would go
to the altar
if she knew all.

Queen Victoria

Happiness is neither virtue nor pleasure nor this thing nor that but simply growth.
We are happy when we are growing.

W.B. Yeats

The game of life is a game of boomerangs. Our thoughts, deeds and words return to us sooner or later with astounding accuracy.

Florence Scovel Shinn

With mirth and laughter let old wrinkles come.

William Shakespeare

As you get older you must remember you have a second hand. The first one is to help yourself. The second hand is to help others.

Audrey Hepburn

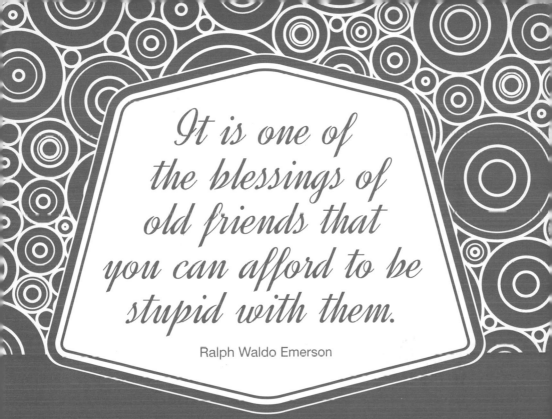

It is one of the blessings of old friends that you can afford to be stupid with them.

Ralph Waldo Emerson

You grow up the day you have your first real laugh at yourself.

Ethel Barrymore

*A lady's imagination is very rapid;
it jumps from admiration to love,
from love to matrimony in a moment.*

Jane Austen

*Time is a
dressmaker
specializing in
alterations.*

Faith Baldwin

To me there is
no picture so
beautiful as smiling,
bright-eyed,
happy children;
no music so sweet
as their clear and
ringing laughter.

P.T. Barnum

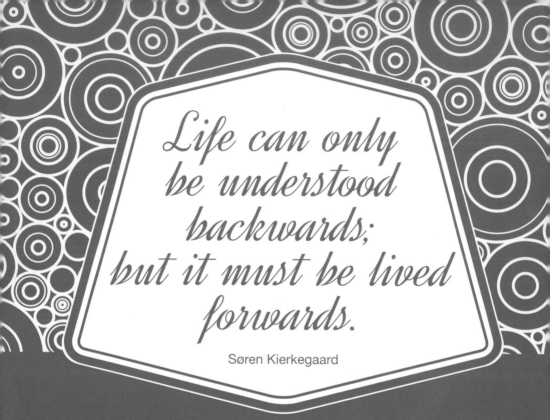

Life can only
be understood
backwards;
but it must be lived
forwards.

Søren Kierkegaard

*Figuring out our gifts in life is part of our journey
to becoming enlightened human beings.*

Allison Dubois

Be happy.
It is one way of being wise.

Colette

*I know enough
to know that
no woman should
ever marry a man
who hated his mother.*

Martha Gellhorn

Laughter is not at all a bad beginning for a friendship, and it is far the best ending for one.

Oscar Wilde

What I've noticed is that almost no one who was a big star in high school is also a big star later in life. For us overlooked kids, it's so wonderfully fair.

Mindy Kaling

Each moment of a happy lover's hour is worth an age of dull and common life.

Aphra Behn

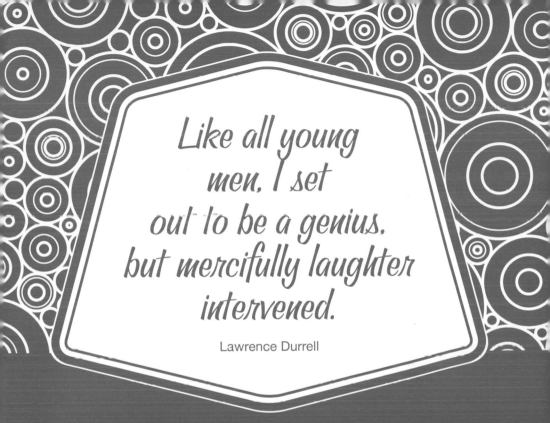

Like all young men, I set out to be a genius, but mercifully laughter intervened.

Lawrence Durrell

The past is never dead. It's not even past.

William Faulkner

How sharper than a
serpent's tooth it is
To have a thankless child!

William Shakespeare

*I am not what
I once was.*

Horace

*People pay for what they do,
and still more for
what they have allowed
themselves to become.
And they pay for it
very simply;
by the lives they lead.*

James Baldwin

To nourish children and raise them against odds is in any time, any place, more valuable than to fix bolts in cars or design nuclear weapons.

Marilyn French

We can never be born enough.

E.E. Cummings

Friends are the family we choose for ourselves.

Edna Buchanan

A woman is always younger than a man at equal years.

Elizabeth Barrett Browning

I was not rescued by a prince;
I was the administrator
of my own rescue.

Elizabeth Gilbert

*You only live once,
but if you do it right,
once is enough.*

Mae West

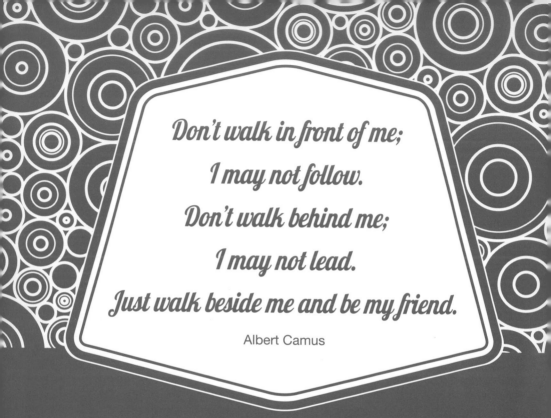

Don't walk in front of me;
I may not follow.
Don't walk behind me;
I may not lead.
Just walk beside me and be my friend.

Albert Camus

I could not, at any age, be content to take my place by the fireside and simply look on. Life was meant to be lived.

Eleanor Roosevelt

To sacrifice what you are and to live without belief, that is a fate more terrible than dying.

Joan of Arc

Life is not a holiday but an education. One eternal lesson for us all: to teach us how better we should love.

Barbara Jordan

It is not a lack of love, but a lack of friendship that makes unhappy marriages.

Friedrich Nietzsche

Snow and adolescence are the only problems that disappear if you ignore them long enough.

Earl Wilson

Our faith in the present dies out long before our faith in the future.

Ruth Benedict

Yes, there's luck in most things; and in none more than being born at the right time.

Edmund Clarence Stedman

Nobody can go back and start a new beginning, but anyone can start today and make a new ending.

Maria Robinson

No, there's nothing half so sweet in life as love's young dream.

Thomas Moore

Many people will walk in and out of your life, but only true friends will leave footprints in your heart.

Eleanor Roosevelt

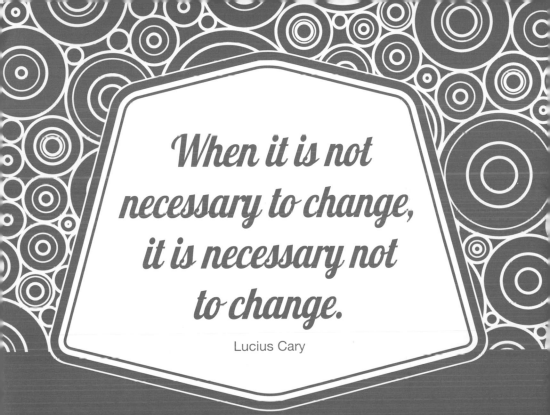

When it is not
necessary to change,
it is necessary not
to change.

Lucius Cary

To teach is to learn twice.

Joseph Joubert

Friendship marks a life
even more deeply than love.
Love risks degenerating into
obsession, friendship is never
anything but sharing.

Elie Wiesel

*One is not born,
but rather becomes,
a woman.*

Simone de Beauvoir

*Sigh no more, ladies,
sigh no more,
Men were deceivers ever;
One foot in sea,
and one on shore,
To one thing
constant never.*

William Shakespeare

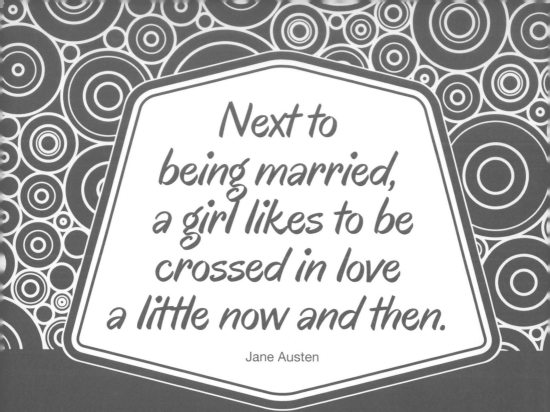

Next to
being married,
a girl likes to be
crossed in love
a little now and then.

Jane Austen

I shall not die of a cold.
I shall die of having lived.

Willa Cather

A mother's happiness
is like a beacon,
lighting up the future
but reflected also
on the past in the
guise of fond memories.

Honoré de Balzac

If there must be trouble, let it be in my day, that my child may have peace.

Thomas Paine

Every man is a quotation from all his ancestors.

Ralph Waldo Emerson

Nothing is more annoying than a low man raised to a high position.

Claudianus

Experience is how life catches up with us and teaches us to love and forgive each other.

Judy Collins

One should take good
care not to grow too wise for so great a
pleasure of life as laughter.

Joseph Addison

Experience: that most
brutal of teachers.
But you learn,
my God do you learn.

C.S. Lewis

*What girls do
to each other
is beyond description.
No Chinese
torture comes close.*

Tori Amos

You could not step twice into the same river; for other waters are ever flowing on to you.

Heraclitus

Better by far you should forget and smile than that you should remember and be sad.

Christina Rossetti

Above our life we love a steadfast friend.

Christopher Marlowe

One must be fond of people and trust them if one is not to make a mess of life.

E.M. Forster

Marriage always demands the finest arts of insincerity possible between two human beings.

Vicki Baum

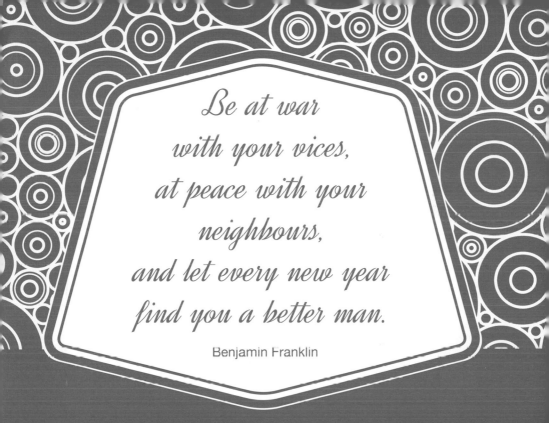

Be at war
with your vices,
at peace with your
neighbours,
and let every new year
find you a better man.

Benjamin Franklin

Every child is an artist. The problem is how to remain an artist once he grows up.

Pablo Picasso

Making the decision to have a child - it's momentous. It is to decide forever to have your heart go walking outside your body.

Elizabeth Stone

Time is what we want most, but what we use worst.

William Penn

Only the actions of the just Smell sweet and blossom in their dust.

James Shirley

As hope and fear alternate chase Our course through life's uncertain race.

Walter Scott

Who is happy? A person who has a healthy body, is dowered with peace of mind, and cultivates his talents.

Thales

No man is in love when he marries.

He may have loved before; I have even heard

he has sometimes loved after:

but at the time never.

Fanny Burney

It's not the years in your life that count, it's the life in your years.

Abraham Lincoln

When the facts change, I change my mind.

John Maynard Keynes

Do not think that years leave us and find us the same!

Owen Meredith

The mind is not a vessel to be filled, but a fire to be ignited.

Plutarch

Happy the man,
and happy he alone,
he who can call today his own;
he who, secure within,
can say, tomorrow
do thy worst,
for I have lived today.

John Dryden

*Women may be the
one group that grows more
radical with age.*

Gloria Steinem

The love we have in
our youth is superficial
compared to the love that an old
man has for his old wife.

Will Durant

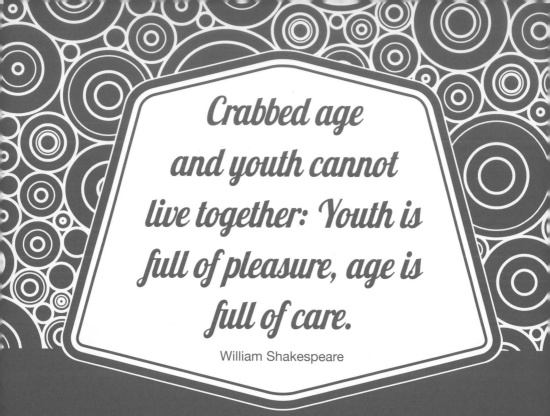

Crabbed age and youth cannot live together: Youth is full of pleasure, age is full of care.

William Shakespeare

Bodies are slow of growth, but are rapid in their dissolution.

Tacitus

Every little girl
knows about love.
It is only her
capacity to
suffer because
of it that increases.

Françoise Sagan

Sweet childish days,
that were as long
As twenty days are now.

William Wordsworth

Children we of
smiles and sighs –
Much we know, but
more we dream.

William Winter

Grave was the man in years, in looks, in word, His locks were grey, yet was his courage green.

Torquato Tasso

Laughter is ever young,
whereas tragedy, except the very
highest of all, quickly becomes haggard.

Margaret Sackville

*To find out what one
is fitted to do, and to secure
an opportunity to do it,
is the key to happiness.*

John Dewey

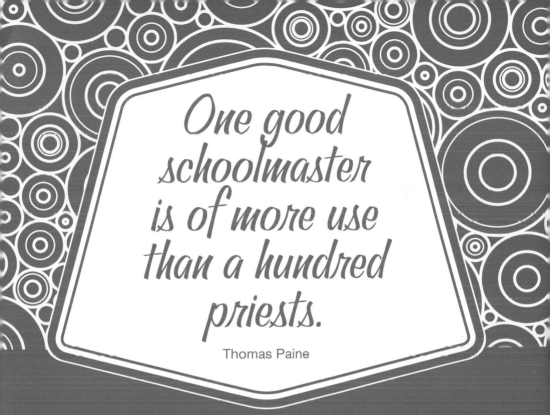

One good schoolmaster is of more use than a hundred priests.

Thomas Paine

Golden lads and girls all must,
As chimney-sweepers, come to dust.

William Shakespeare

What a wonderful life I've had! I only wish I'd realized it sooner.

Colette

The Wide World

To travel is to discover that everyone is wrong about other countries.

Aldous Huxley

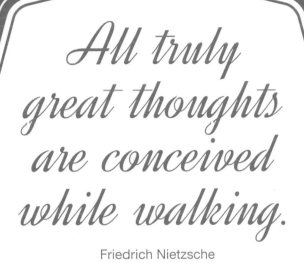

All truly great thoughts are conceived while walking.

Friedrich Nietzsche

Travel makes a wise man better,
and a fool worse.

Thomas Fuller

In wilderness I sense the miracle of life, and behind it our scientific accomplishments fade to trivia.

Charles A. Lindbergh

For whatever we lose
(like a you or a me),
It's always our self we find in the sea.

E.E. Cummings

It is not easy
to walk alone in the
country without musing
upon something.

Charles Dickens

Not all who wander are lost.

J.R.R. Tolkien

The most beautiful thing we can experience is the mysterious. It is the source of all true art and science.

Albert Einstein

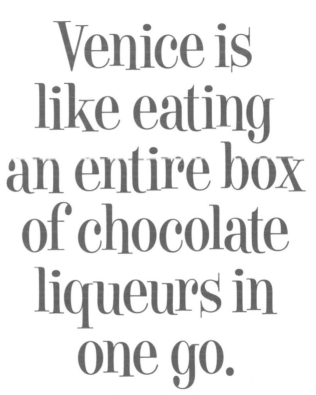

Venice is like eating an entire box of chocolate liqueurs in one go.

Truman Capote

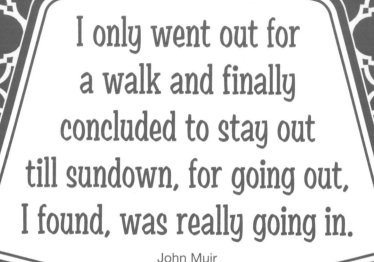

I only went out for
a walk and finally
concluded to stay out
till sundown, for going out,
I found, was really going in.

John Muir

Travel is glamorous only in retrospect.

Paul Theroux

One does not meet
oneself until one
catches the
reflection
from an eye
other than
human.

Loren Eiseley

My country is the world and my religion is to do good.

Thomas Paine

A journey is like marriage. The certain way to be wrong is to think you control it.

John Steinbeck

I wonder anybody does anything at Oxford but dream and remember, the place is so beautiful.

W.B. Yeats

The first condition of understanding a foreign country is to smell it.

Rudyard Kipling

They sicken of the calm who know the storm.

Dorothy Parker

The world is
all about you:
you can fence
yourselves in,
but you cannot
for ever fence
it out.

J.R.R. Tolkien

*What humbugs we are,
who pretend to live for Beauty,
and never see the Dawn!*

Logan Pearsall Smith

The true secret of happiness lies in taking a genuine interest in all the details of daily life.

William Morris

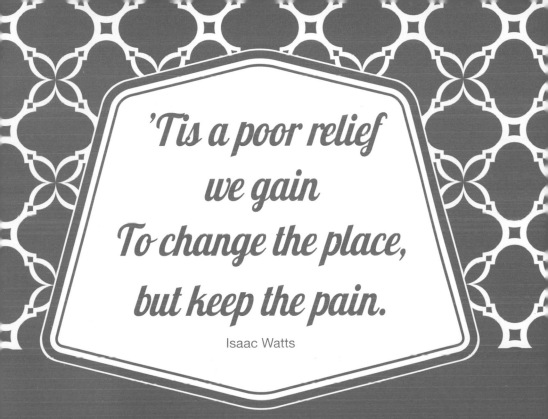

'Tis a poor relief
we gain
To change the place,
but keep the pain.

Isaac Watts

All things change, nothing perishes.

Ovid

Stop shallow water still running, it will rage; tread on a worm and it will turn.

Robert Greene

One can find so many pains when the rain is falling.

John Steinbeck

When I no longer thrill to the first snow of the season, I'll know I'm growing old.

Lady Bird Johnson

You can't be
suspicious of
a tree, or accuse a
bird or a squirrel
of subversion
or challenge the
ideology of
a violet.

Hal Borland

I heard the old, old men say,
'All that's beautiful drifts away,
Like the waters.'

W.B. Yeats

Too often travel, instead of broadening the mind, merely lengthens the conversations.

Elizabeth Drew

Trees outstrip most people in the extent and depth of their work for the public good

Sara Ebenreck

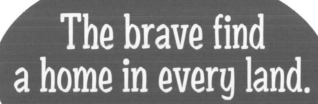

The brave find
a home in every land.

Ovid

There is more stupidity
than hydrogen in
the universe, and it has
a longer shelf life.

Frank Zappa

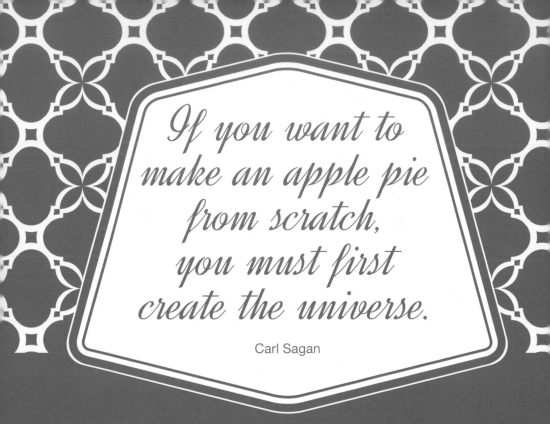

If you want to make an apple pie from scratch, you must first create the universe.

Carl Sagan

Go to heaven for the climate and hell for the company.

Mark Twain

I moved to New York City
for my health.
I'm paranoid and
New York was
the only place
where my fears were
justified.

Anita Weiss

I feel about airplanes the way I feel about diets: it seems to me that they are wonderful things for other people to go on.

Jean Kerr

I am not a vegetarian because I love animals; I am a vegetarian because I hate plants.

A. Whitney Brown

*Adults are always
so busy with the dull
and dusty affairs
of life which have
nothing to do with
grass, trees, and
running streams.*

Denys Watkins-Pitchford

I grew up in Europe, where the history comes from.

Eddie Izzard

If there is magic on this planet, it is contained in water.

Loren Eiseley

There's a magical tie to the land of our home, which the heart cannot break, though the footsteps may roam.

Eliza Cook

The coldest winter I ever spent was a summer in San Francisco.

Mark Twain

Nature does not hurry, yet everything is accomplished.

Lao Tzu

The universe seems neither benign nor hostile, merely indifferent.

Carl Sagan

The sky is that beautiful old parchment in which the sun and the moon keep their diary.

Alfred Kreymborg

What makes the desert beautiful is that somewhere it hides a well.

Antoine de Saint-Exupéry

He is no wise man that will quit a certainty for an uncertainty.

Samuel Johnson

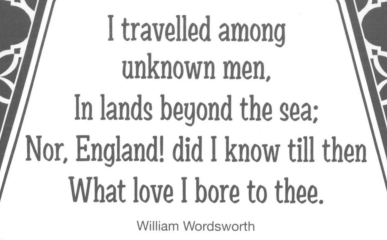

I travelled among
unknown men,
In lands beyond the sea;
Nor, England! did I know till then
What love I bore to thee.

William Wordsworth

A lawn is nature under totalitarian rule.

Michael Pollan

Travel, in the younger sort, is a part of education; in the elder, a part of experience.

Francis Bacon

France is France and a grand place for Frenchmen.

Harry Truman

You can fall in love at first sight with a place as with a person.

Alec Waugh

To be interested in the changing seasons is a happier state of mind than to be hopelessly in love with spring.

George Santayana

There are 6 million interesting people in New York, and 72 in Los Angeles.

Neil Simon

Look deep into nature,
and then you
will understand
everything better.

Albert Einstein

No one but Night,
with tears on her dark face,
Watches beside me in
this windy place.

Edna St Vincent Millay

Truly it may be said
that the outside
of a mountain
is good for the
inside of a man.

George Wherry

*Who is staring
at the sea is already
sailing a little.*

Paul Carvel

Every age has
its pleasures, its
style of wit, and
its own ways.

Nicholas Boileau-Despréaux

We shall not cease from
exploration
And at the end of all our
exploring
Will be to arrive where
we started
And know the place for
the first time.

T.S. Eliot

Nature never
deceives us;
it is we who
deceive ourselves.

Jean-Jacques Rousseau

Poor Mexico, so far from God and so close to the United States!

Porfirio Díaz

Certain dank gardens cry aloud for a murder; certain old houses demand to be haunted; certain coasts are set apart for shipwrecks.

Robert Louis Stevenson

The clouds,
the only birds
that never sleep.

Victor Hugo

The earth has music for those who listen.

William Shakespeare

God made the country, and man made the town.

William Cowper

Nature is inside art as its content, not outside as its model.

Marilyn French

A happy life must be to a great extent a quiet life, for it is only in an atmosphere of quiet that true joy dare live.

Bertrand Russell

He is happiest, be he king or peasant, who finds peace in his home.

Johann Wolfgang von Goethe

Let us enjoy pleasure while we can; pleasure is never long enough.

Sextus Propertius

I have no relish for the country; it is a kind of healthy grave.

Sydney Smith

Travelling tends to magnify all human emotions.

Peter Høeg

It is good to have an end to journey toward; but it is the journey that matters, in the end.

Ursula Le Guin

To provide meaningful architecture is not to parody history but to articulate it.

Daniel Libeskind

Study nature, love nature, stay close to nature. It will never fail you.

Frank Lloyd Wright

Eden is that
old-fashioned
house we dwell
in every day
Without suspecting
our abode until
we drive away.

Emily Dickinson

Stuff your eyes with wonder,
live as if you'd drop
dead in ten seconds.
See the world.
It's more fantastic than
any dream made or paid for
in factories.

Ray Bradbury

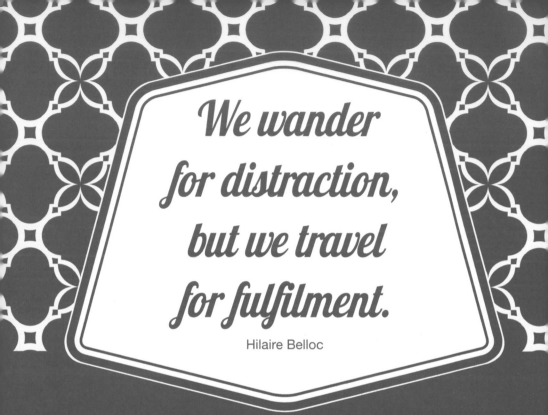

We wander for distraction, but we travel for fulfilment.

Hilaire Belloc

When snow falls, nature listens.

Antoinette van Kleeff

The soul should always stand ajar, ready to welcome the ecstatic experience.

Emily Dickinson

Nature's far too subtle to repeat herself.

Paul Muni

I freed a thousand slaves. I could have freed a thousand more if only they knew they were slaves.

Harriet Tubman

The real voyage of discovery consists not in seeking new landscapes, but in having new eyes.

Marcel Proust

A harmonious design requires that nothing be added or taken away.

Marcus Vitruvius Pollio

Anybody can be good in the country.

Oscar Wilde

If you want to build a ship, don't drum up the men to gather wood, divide the work, and give orders. Instead, teach them to yearn for the vast and endless sea.

Antoine de Saint-Exupéry

The first fall of snow is not only an event, it is a magical event. You go to bed in one kind of world and wake up in another quite different, and if this is not enchantment then where is it to be found?

J.B. Priestley

The great
thing about
being an
architect is you
can walk into
your dreams.

Harold E. Wagoner

The traveller sees what he sees, the tourist sees what he has come to see.

G.K. Chesterton

Travel teaches toleration.

Benjamin Disraeli

We cannot in one lifetime see all that we would like to see or to learn all that we hunger to know.

Loren Eiseley

Things forbidden have a secret charm.

Tacitus

I roamed the countryside searching for answers to things I did not understand.

Leonardo da Vinci

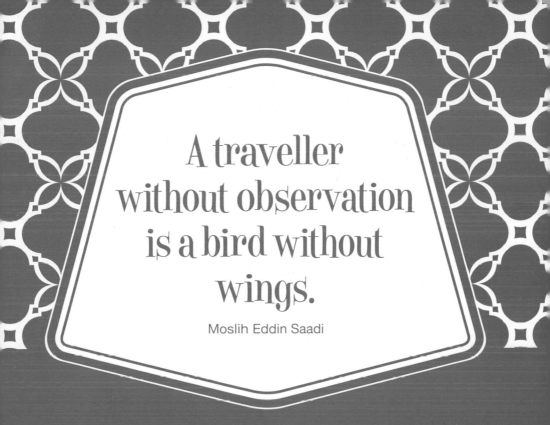

A traveller without observation is a bird without wings.

Moslih Eddin Saadi

Architecture is petrified music.

Felix E. Schelling

The worst of a modern stylish mansion is that it has no place for ghosts.

Oliver Wendell Holmes

The supreme happiness of life is the conviction that we are loved; loved for ourselves, or rather in spite of ourselves.

Victor Hugo

All of us were born for one another.

Marcus Aurelius

No man is an island, entire of itself.

John Donne

No one is useless in the world who lightens the burdens of another.

Charles Dickens

Injustice anywhere is a threat to justice everywhere.

Martin Luther King

Peace is the first thing the angels sang.

John Keble

Love is when he gives you a piece of your soul that you never knew was missing.

Torquato Tasso

I think there's just one kind of folks. Folks.

Harper Lee

When everyone agrees, someone is not thinking.

General George S. Patton

Love is a better teacher than duty.

Albert Einstein

Love makes your soul crawl out from its hiding place.

Zora Neale Hurston

Love is life's end,
but never ending.
Love is life's wealth,
never spent,
but ever spending.
Love's life's reward,
rewarded in rewarding.

Herbert Spencer

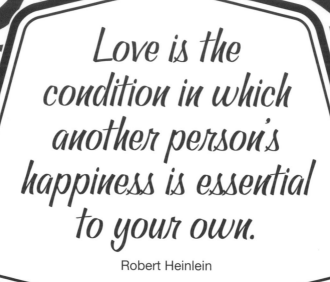

Love is the condition in which another person's happiness is essential to your own.

Robert Heinlein

Peace is rarely denied to the peaceful.

Friedrich Schiller

The truth is, everyone is going to hurt you. You just got to find the ones worth suffering for.

Bob Marley

Can miles truly separate you from friends . . . If you want to be with someone you love, aren't you already there?

Richard Bach

Love is always bestowed as a gift - freely, willingly and without expectation. We don't love to be loved; we love to love.

Leo Buscaglia

To fear love is to fear life, and those who fear life are already three parts dead.

Bertrand Russell

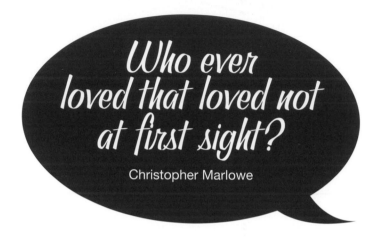

Who ever loved that loved not at first sight?

Christopher Marlowe

The way to love anything is to realize that it may be lost.

G.K. Chesterton

Be not dishearten'd.
Affection shall solve the
problems of Freedom yet;
Those who love each other
shall become invincible.

Walt Whitman

Resist much. Obey little.

Walt Whitman

143

Love means to commit yourself without guarantee.

Anne Campbell

Temptation is a woman's weapon and a man's excuse.

H.L. Mencken

It's useless to hold
a person to anything
he says while he's
in love, drunk, or
running for office.

Shirley MacLaine

Non-violence doesn't always work — but violence never does.

Madge Michaels-Cyrus

Love ceases to be a pleasure when it ceases to be a secret.

Aphra Behn

It is doubtful if
any gift could be bought
more precious than
the adoration of a heart
which has put out
all hatred, self-pity and
desire for revenge.

Charlotte Brontë

I like not only to be loved, but also to be told I am loved.

George Eliot

When love is not madness, it is not love.

Pedro Calderon de la Barca

The stars may be large, but they cannot think or love.

F.P. Ramsey

To love another person is to see the face of God.

Victor Hugo

Love is when
you meet someone
who tells you
something new about
yourself.

André Breton

We can only learn to love by loving.

Iris Murdoch

To love abundantly is to live abundantly, and to love forever is to live forever.

Henry Drummond

The truth is cruel, but it can be loved, and it makes free those who have loved it.

George Santayana

Love takes off masks that we fear we cannot live without and know we cannot live within.

James Baldwin

What the world really needs is more love and less paperwork.

Pearl Bailey

A friend to all is a friend to none.

Aristotle

I dream of giving birth to a child who will ask: 'Mother, what was war?'

Eve Merriam

I don't need a friend who nods when I nod, and who changes when I change. My shadow does that much better.

Plutarch

Pains of love be sweeter far than all other pleasures are.

John Dryden

To love for the sake of being loved is human, but to love for the sake of loving is angelic.

Alphonse de Lamartine

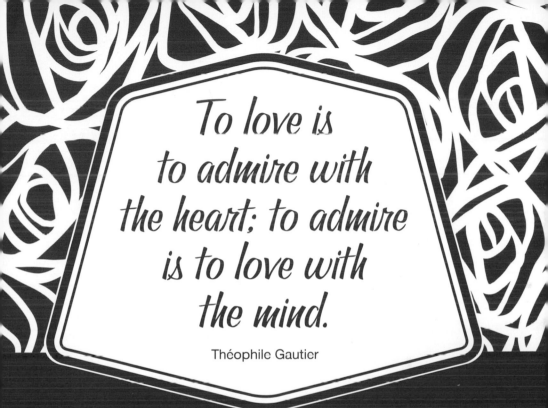

To love is
to admire with
the heart; to admire
is to love with
the mind.

Théophile Gautier

Love is a hole in the heart.

Ben Hecht

Women need to feel loved and men need to feel needed.

Rita Mae Brown

Love never claims, it ever gives. Love ever suffers, never resents, never revenges itself.

Mahatma Gandhi

If my love was a well, you would never go thirsty. If my love was a fire, you would never be cold. If my love was a star, you would never be left in the dark.

Francisco Garcia

Courageous people do not fear forgiving, for the sake of peace.

Nelson Mandela

Be kind, for everyone you meet is fighting a hard battle.

Seneca

The spring of love becomes hidden and soon filled up.

Max Muller

Sharing is sometimes more demanding than giving.

Mary Catherine Bateson

Let no man pull you low enough to hate him.

Martin Luther King, Jr.

The deep joy we take in the company of people with whom we have just recently fallen in love is undisguisable.

John Cheever

Let us be grateful to people who make us happy, they are the charming gardeners who make our souls blossom.

Marcel Proust

Words may be false and full of art; Sighs are the natural language of the heart.

Thomas Shadwell

It's the friends you can call up at 4 a.m. that matter.

Marlene Dietrich

*Be brave, young lovers,
and follow your star.*

Oscar Hammerstein II

Love is an act of
endless forgiveness,
a tender look which
becomes a habit.

Peter Ustinov

If everyone demanded peace instead of another television set, then there'd be peace.

John Lennon

A successful marriage requires falling in love many times, always with the same person.

Mignon McLaughlin

The best thing to hold onto in life is each other.

Audrey Hepburn

Love is our response to our highest values – and can be nothing else.

Ayn Rand

When the power of love overcomes the love of power, the world will know peace.

Jimi Hendrix

*Bid me
to love, and I
will give a loving
heart to thee.*

Robert Herrick

Do all things with love.

Og Mandino

I have never met a person whose greatest need was anything other than real, unconditional love. You can find it in a simple act of kindness towards someone who needs help.

Elisabeth Kübler-Ross

Hell is yourself and the only redemption is when a person puts himself aside to feel deeply for another person.

Tennessee Williams

There is never a time or place for true love. It happens accidentally, in a heartbeat, in a single flashing, throbbing moment.

Sarah Dessen

It is easier to love humanity as a whole than to love one's neighbour.

Eric Hoffer

If you can make a woman laugh, you can make her do anything.

Marilyn Monroe

I love you as certain
dark things are to
be loved, in secret,
between the shadow
and the soul.

Pablo Neruda

So, I love you because the entire universe conspired to help me find you.

Paulo Coelho

Love each other or perish.

W.H. Auden

Love is a fire. But whether it is going to warm your hearth or burn down your house, you can never tell.

Joan Crawford

The words of kindness are more healing to a drooping heart than balm or honey.

Sarah Fielding

A real friend is one who walks in when the rest of the world walks out.

Walter Winchell

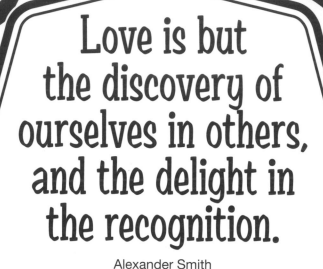

Love is but
the discovery of
ourselves in others,
and the delight in
the recognition.

Alexander Smith

The course of true
love never did run smooth.

William Shakespeare

Sometimes love means letting go when you want to hold on tighter.

Melissa Marr

There is nothing I
would not do for
those who are really
my friends. I have
no notion of loving
people by halves, it is
not my nature.

Jane Austen

If we would build
on a sure foundation
in friendship we
must love friends
for their sake rather
than our own.

Charlotte Brontë

Mother's love is peace. It need not be acquired, it need not be deserved.

Erich Fromm

Love doesn't make the world go round; love is what makes the ride worthwhile.

Franklin P. Jones

You can't measure the mutual affection of two human beings by the number of words they exchange.

Milan Kundera

The man of knowledge
must be able
not only to
love his enemies
but also to
hate his friends.

Friedrich Nietzsche

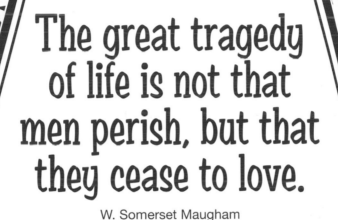

The great tragedy
of life is not that
men perish, but that
they cease to love.

W. Somerset Maugham

It is only in the giving of oneself
to others that we truly live.

Ethel Percy Andrus

I can live without money, but I cannot live without love.

Judy Garland

I am weird, you are weird. Everyone in this world is weird. One day two people come together in mutual weirdness and fall in love.

Dr Seuss

I would like to be the air that inhabits you for a moment only. I would like to be that unnoticed and that necessary.

Margaret Atwood

It took us so long
to realize that a
purpose of human
life, no matter who is
controlling it, is to love
whoever is around to
be loved.

Kurt Vonnegut

Love one another but make not a bond of love: let it rather be a moving sea between the shores of your souls.

Khalil Gibran

What is done in love is done well.

Vincent Van Gogh

What do we live for, if it is not to make life less difficult for each other?

George Eliot

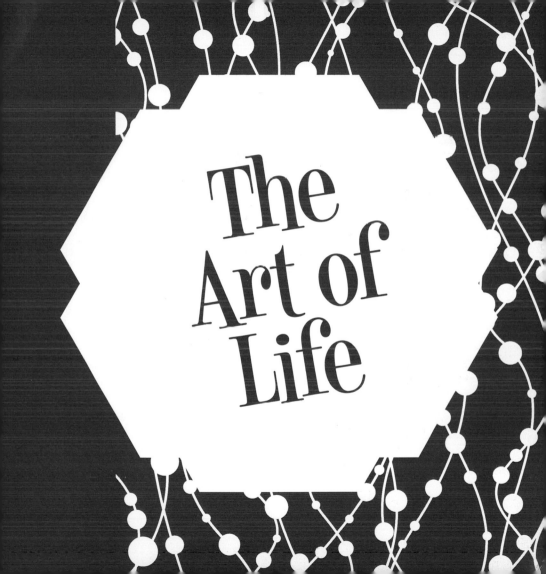

Every artist dips his brush in his own soul, and paints his own nature into his pictures.

Henry Ward Beecher

To draw, you must close your eyes and sing.

Pablo Picasso

Many people would die sooner than think; in fact, they do.

Bertrand Russell

You can't depend
on your eyes when your
imagination is out of focus.

Mark Twain

*I look to the future
because that's where
I'm going to spend the
rest of my life.*

George Burns

Comment is free, but facts are sacred.

C.P. Scott

*It is now life
and not art
that requires
the willing
suspension of
disbelief.*

Lionel Trilling

This is the artist, then,
life's hungry man,
the glutton of eternity,
beauty's miser,
glory's slave.

Thomas Wolfe

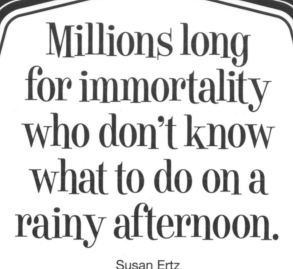

Millions long
for immortality
who don't know
what to do on a
rainy afternoon.

Susan Ertz

Be true to your work, your word,
and your friend.

Henry David Thoreau

Creativity is allowing yourself to make mistakes. Art is knowing which ones to keep.

Scott Adams

I was irrevocably betrothed to laughter, the sound of which has always seemed to me the most civilized music in the world.

Peter Ustinov

202

Draw your pleasure,
paint your pleasure,
and express your pleasure
strongly.

Pierre Bonnard

*Any activity
becomes creative when
the doer cares about doing
it right or better.*

John Updike

This will be our reply to violence: to make music more intensely, more beautifully, more devotedly than ever before.

Leonard Bernstein

Inspiration could be called inhaling the memory of an act never experienced.

Ned Rorem

*Art is when you
hear a knocking from your
soul - and you answer.*

Terri Guillemets

*The poet makes himself a seer
by a long, prodigious and rational
disordering of all the senses.*

Arthur Rimbaud

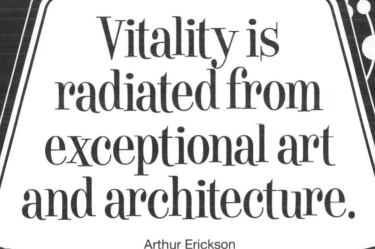

Vitality is radiated from exceptional art and architecture.

Arthur Erickson

The world is but a canvas to the imagination.

Henry David Thoreau

You can't deny laughter; when it comes, it plops down in your favourite chair and stays as long as it wants.

Stephen King

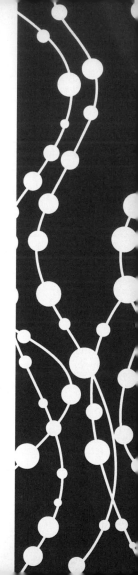

Always have a book. Always have a movie. Always have a notebook. And then always have a sense of humour.

Phil Keoghan

A likely impossibility is always preferable to an unconvincing possibility.

Aristotle

True art takes note not merely of form but also of what lies behind.

Mahatma Gandhi

Anxiety is the handmaiden of creativity.

Chuck Jones

I don't need a bedroom to prove my womanliness. I can convey just as much sex appeal picking apples off a tree or standing in the rain.

Audrey Hepburn

There is no greater agony than bearing an untold story inside you.

Maya Angelou

What is done in love is done well.

Vincent Van Gogh

Laughter is one of the very privileges of reason, being confined to the human species.

Thomas Carlyle

The best way to have a good idea is to have lots of ideas.

Linus Pauling

Genius is one per cent inspiration, ninety-nine per cent perspiration.

Thomas Edison

Humour has justly been regarded as the finest perfection of poetic genius.

Thomas Carlyle

You don't have
to burn books to
destroy a culture.
Just get people
to stop reading
them.

Ray Bradbury

A wise man proportions his belief to the evidence.

David Hume

As music is the poetry of sound,
so is painting the poetry of sight.

James McNeil Whistler

Do not be troubled for a language, cultivate your soul and she will show herself.

Eugene Delacroix

The muscles of writing are not so visible, but they are just as powerful: determination, attention, curiosity, a passionate heart.

Natalie Goldberg

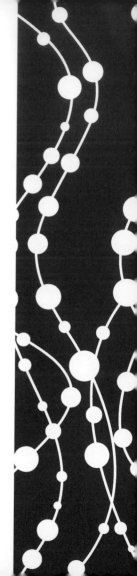

It's better to fail in originality, than succeed in imitation.

Herman Melville

Creative thinking is not a talent, it is a skill that can be learnt. It empowers people by adding strength to their natural abilities.

Edward de Bono

You can't use up creativity. The more you use, the more you have.

Maya Angelou

Fill your paper with the breathings of your heart.

William Wordsworth

To me, the greatest pleasure of writing is not what it's about, but the inner music the words make.

Truman Capote

*It is better to write
of laughter than
of tears,
for laughter
is the property
of man.*

François Rabelais

Great minds discuss ideas. Average minds discuss events. Small minds discuss people.

Eleanor Roosevelt

I don't paint to live, I live to paint.

Willem de Kooning

The act of painting is about one heart telling another heart where he found salvation.

Francisco Goya

Only passions, and great passions, can raise the soul to great things.

Denis Diderot

At some point in life
the world's beauty
becomes enough.
You don't need to
photograph, paint,
or even remember it.
It is enough.

Toni Morrison

Art has to move you and design does not, unless it's a good design for a bus.

David Hockney

Art is a collaboration between God and the artist, and the less the artist does the better.

André Gide

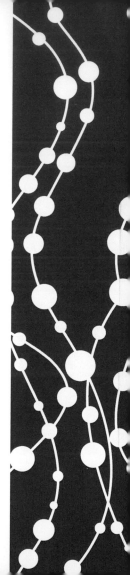

Poetry and Hums aren't things which you get, they're things which get you. And all you can do is to go where they can find you.

A.A. Milne

The creative mind plays with the object it loves.

Carl Jung

No idea is so outlandish that it should not be considered with a searching but at the same time steady eye.

Winston Churchill

There is nothing either good or bad, but thinking makes it so.

William Shakespeare

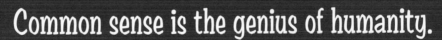

Common sense is the genius of humanity.

Johann Wolfgang von Goethe

Your words are the greatest power you have. The words you choose and their use establish the life you experience.

Sonia Choquette

In a time of universal deceit, telling the truth becomes a revolutionary act.

George Orwell

Everything has been thought of before, but the problem is to think of it again.

Johann Wolfgang von Goethe

One day we'll all find out that all of our songs were just little notes in a great big song.

Woody Guthrie

You can't wait
for inspiration.
Sometimes you have to
go after it with a club.

Jack London

Art attracts us only by
what it reveals of our
most secret self.

Jean-Luc Godard

Creative activity could be described as a type of learning process where teacher and pupil are located in the same individual.

Arthur Koestler

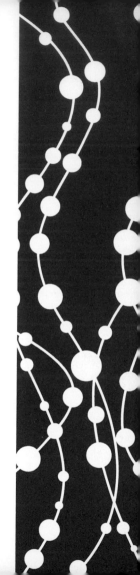

The only difference between an artist and a lunatic is, perhaps, that the artist has the restraint or courtesy to conceal the intensity of his obsession from all except those similarly afflicted.

Osbert Sitwell

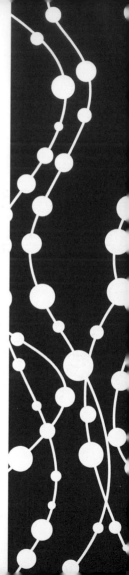

The difference between the right word and the almost right word is the difference between lightning and a lightning bug.

Mark Twain

Every painting is a voyage into a sacred harbour.

Giotto di Bondone

No one has ever written, painted, sculpted, modelled, built or invented except literally to get out of hell.

Antonin Artaud

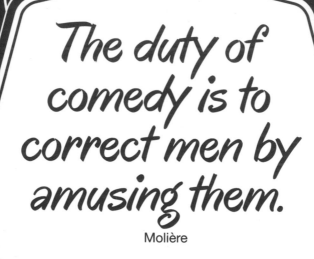

The duty of comedy is to correct men by amusing them.

Molière

Don't think about making art, just get it done.

Andy Warhol

Creativity is the sudden cessation of stupidity.

Edwin H. Land

A statue has never been set up in honour of a critic.

Jean Sibelius

Life is infinitely stranger than anything which the mind of man could invent.

Arthur Conan Doyle

To imagine is everything, to know is nothing at all.

Anatole France

I write only because there is a voice within me that will not be still.

Sylvia Plath

You can take all the sincerity in Hollywood, place it in the navel of a fruit fly and still have room enough for three caraway seeds and a producer's heart.

Fred Allen

*Without craft,
art remains private.
Without art, craft is
merely hackwork.*

Joyce Carol Oates

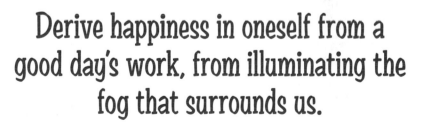

Derive happiness in oneself from a
good day's work, from illuminating the
fog that surrounds us.

Henri Matisse

You may not be
a Picasso or Mozart
but you don't have to be.
Just create to create.
Create to remind yourself
you're still alive.

Frederick Terral

Painting is silent poetry, and poetry is painting that speaks.

Plutarch

Inspiration exists, but it must find you working.

Pablo Picasso

Everything should be made as simple as possible, but not simpler.

Albert Einstein

Humour is by far the most significant activity of the human brain.

Edward de Bono

No good opera plot can
be sensible, for people do not
sing when they are sensible.

W.H. Auden

Those who do not
want to imitate anything,
produce nothing.

Salvador Dali

If I create from the heart,
nearly everything works;
if from the head,
almost nothing.

Marc Chagall

Read in order to live.

Gustave Flaubert

True storytelling reveals meaning without committing the error of defining it.

Hannah Arendt

I don't wait for moods. You accomplish nothing if you do that. Your mind must know it has got to get down to work.

Pearl S. Buck

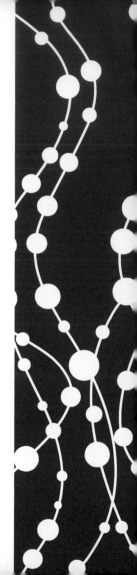

For most of history, Anonymous was a woman.

Virginia Woolf

The essence of all beautiful art, all great art, is gratitude.

Friedrich Nietzsche

Being an author is having angels whisper in your ear - and devils, too.

Graycie Harmon

All you really have that really matters are feelings. That's what music is to me.

Janis Joplin

One can live in the shadow of an idea without grasping it.

Elizabeth Bowen

Life is a jest, and all things show it, I thought so once, and now I know it.

John Gay

Being willing is not enough; we must do.

Leonardo da Vinci

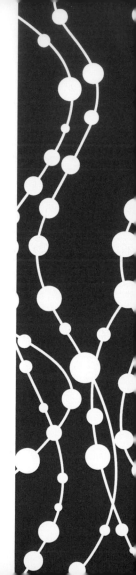

The mind once enlightened cannot again become dark.

Thomas Paine

Three things cannot long be hidden: the sun, the moon, and the truth.

Confucius

Success
and
Failure

Fetters of gold are still fetters, and the softest lining can never make them so easy as liberty.

Mary Astell

Life is what happens to you while you're busy making other plans.

Allen Saunders

Character is much easier kept than recovered.

Thomas Paine

Misfortune, and recited misfortune especially, can be prolonged to the point where it ceases to excite pity and arouses only irritation.

Dorothy Parker

To be truly radical is to make hope possible rather than despair convincing.

Raymond Williams

To be without some of the things you want is an indispensable part of happiness.

Bertrand Russell

Problems cannot be solved by thinking within the framework in which they were created.

Albert Einstein

The winds and waves are always on the side of the ablest navigators.

Edward Gibbon

I am where I am because I believe in all possibilities.

Whoopi Goldberg

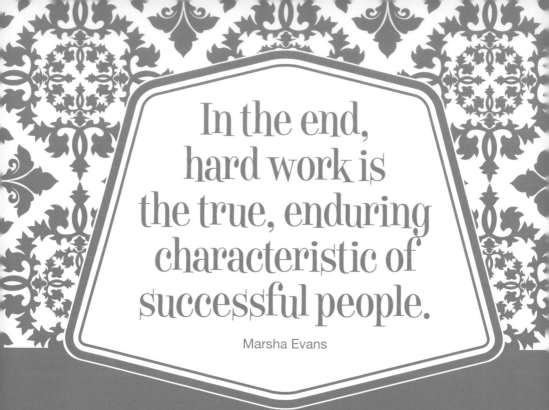

In the end,
hard work is
the true, enduring
characteristic of
successful people.

Marsha Evans

Of course I believe in luck. How otherwise to
explain the success of some people you detest?

Jean Cocteau

Nor need we power or
splendour, wide hall
or lordly dome;
The good,
the true,
the tender -
these form the
wealth of home.

Sarah J. Hale

Unseen in the background, Fate was quietly slipping lead into the boxing-glove.

P.G. Wodehouse

Luck to me is . . . realizing what is opportunity and what isn't.

Lucille Ball

This time, like all times, is a very good one if we but know what to do with it.

Ralph Waldo Emerson

Success and Failure

Patience is what you must have when you don't have luck.

Tennessee Williams

*Failure?
I never encountered it.
All I ever met were
temporary setbacks.*

Dottie Walters

I know I have
but the body of a
weak and feeble
woman, but I have
the heart and
stomach of a king,
and of a king of
England, too.

Elizabeth I

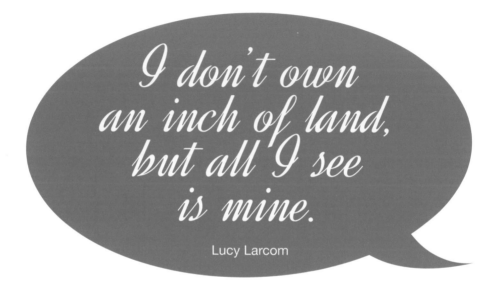

*I don't own
an inch of land,
but all I see
is mine.*

Lucy Larcom

Sometimes it's worse to win a fight than to lose.

Billie Holiday

We are what
we repeatedly do.
Excellence, then,
is not an act but
a habit.

Aristotle

Prosperity is full of friends.

Euripides

When you are unhappy, is there anything more maddening than to be told that you should be contented with your lot?

Kathleen Norris

In struggling against anguish one never produces serenity; the struggle against anguish only produces new forms of anguish.

Simone Weil

There is nothing upon
the face of the earth
so insipid as a medium.
Give me love or hate!
A friend that will go
to jail for me, or an
enemy that will run
me through the body!

Fanny Burney

Some people are so fond of bad luck they run half way to meet it.

Douglas William Jerrold

No one has ever become poor by giving.

Anne Frank

When you lose a couple of times, it makes you realize how difficult it is to win.

Steffi Graf

The worst cynicism: a belief in luck.

Joyce Carol Oates

Success is not the key to happiness. Happiness is the key to success. If you love what you are doing, you will be successful.

Albert Schweitzer

Whatever you do,
be different - that was
the advice my mother
gave me, and I can't
think of better advice for
an entrepreneur.
If you're different, you
will stand out.

Anita Roddick

*Nothing is as obnoxious
as other people's luck.*

F. Scott Fitzgerald

*Courage is
the price that life exacts
for granting peace.*

Amelia Earhart

*Don't feel entitled
to anything you
didn't sweat and
struggle for.*

Marian Wright Edelman

My friends are my estate.

Emily Dickinson

Any woman who understands the problems of running a home will be nearer to understanding the problems of running a country.

Margaret Thatcher

A crust eaten in peace is better than a banquet partaken in anxiety.

Aesop

It is our choices that show what we truly are, far more than our abilities.

J.K. Rowling

Greatness is not measured by what a man or woman accomplishes, but by the opposition he or she has overcome to reach his or her goals.

Dorothy Height

Excellence is doing ordinary things extraordinarily well.

John W. Gardner

Failures are either those who do not know what they want or are not prepared to pay the price asked them.

W.H. Auden

We need greater
virtues to sustain
good fortune
than bad.

François de La Rouchefoucauld

Success breeds confidence.

Beryl Markham

Everything that comes to us from chance is unstable, and the higher it rises, the more liable it is to fall.

Seneca

Any fool can have bad luck; the art consists in knowing how to exploit it.

Frank Wedekind

I've lost almost 300 games. 26 times I've been trusted to take the game-winning shot and missed. I've failed over and over and over again in my life. And that is why I succeed.

Michael Jordan

Human successes,
like human failures,
are composed of
one action at a time
and achieved by one
person at a time.

Patsy H. Sampson

The secret of getting ahead is getting started.

Sally Berger

To a brave man, good and bad luck are like his right and left hand. He uses both.

St Catherine of Siena

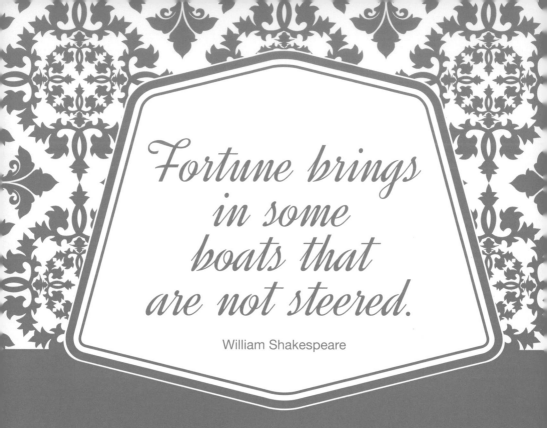

Fortune brings in some boats that are not steered.

William Shakespeare

Buying is a profound pleasure.

Simone de Beauvoir

The day, water, sun, moon, night - I do not have to purchase these things with money.

Plautus

We are never so happy nor so unhappy as we imagine.

François de La Rouchefoucauld

To desire nothing beyond what you have is surely happiness.

Carleton Mitchell

Take rest;
a field that has
rested gives a
bountiful crop.

Ovid

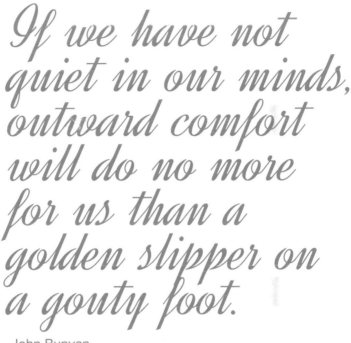

If we have not quiet in our minds, outward comfort will do no more for us than a golden slipper on a gouty foot.

John Bunyan

There is no pleasure in having nothing to do; the fun is in having lots to do and not doing it.

Mary Wilson Little

Being defeated is often a temporary condition. Giving up is what makes it permanent.

Marilyn Von Savant

You know, you do need mentors, but in the end, you really just need to believe in yourself.

Diana Ross

A man is a success if he gets up in the morning and goes to bed at night and in between does what he wants to do.

Bob Dylan

Destiny is a good thing to accept when it's going your way. When it isn't, don't call it destiny; call it injustice, treachery, or simple bad luck.

Joseph Heller

When life is too easy for us, we must beware or we may not be ready to meet the blows which sooner or later come to everyone, rich or poor.

Eleanor Roosevelt

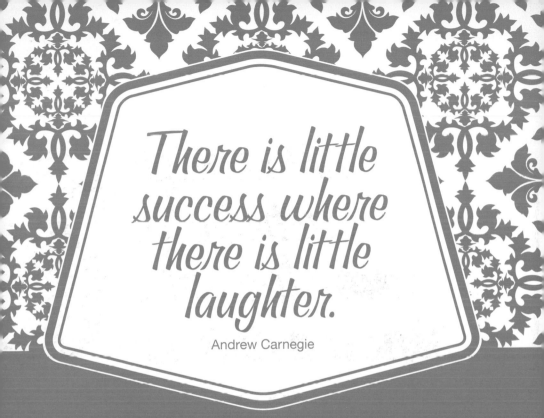

There is little success where there is little laughter.

Andrew Carnegie

Fail, fail again, fail better.

Samuel Beckett

It is not enough to be busy. So are the ants. The question is: What are we busy about?

Henry David Thoreau

It is not very often that an opportunity comes knocking. But when it does, you better be bathed and dressed and ready to answer its call.

Jyoti Arora

If we are not grateful,
then no matter how
much we have we
will not be happy -
because we will
always want to
have something
else or something more.

David Steindl-Rast

*Luck is not chance,
it's toil;
fortune's expensive smile
is earned.*

Emily Dickinson

It was, perhaps, one of those cases in which advice is good or bad only as the event decides.

Jane Austen

Sadness and love and pain, they're easy to feel — but not luck.

Sophie. D. Crockett

If you're not failing every now and again, it's a sign you're not doing anything very innovative.

Woody Allen

Winning isn't everything, but wanting to win is.

Vince Lombardi

Life is not a matter
of holding good cards,
but of playing a
poor hand well.

Robert Louis Stevenson

It never rains but it pours.

Lucy Maud Montgomery

Great people know how to take care of their people. For a great person does not become great by themselves.

John Maeda

People always call it luck when you've acted more sensibly than they have.

Anne Tyler

A woman's always safe and comfortable when a fellow's down on his luck.

Louisa May Alcott

There is only one real deprivation . . . and that is not to be able to give one's gifts to those one loves most.

May Sarton

Sometimes your joy is the source of your smile, but sometimes your smile can be the source of your joy.

Thích Nhat Hanh

Don't agonize, organize.

Florynce Kennedy

In the face of an obstacle which is impossible to overcome, stubbornness is stupid.

Simone de Beauvoir

From quiet homes and
first beginning,
Out to the
undiscovered ends,
There's nothing worth
the wear of winning,
But laughter and the
love of friends.

Hilaire Belloc

The secret of happiness is
to admire without desiring.

Carl Sandburg

*The only way
to do great
work is to
love what you do.*

Steve Jobs

What we obtain too cheap, we esteem too lightly: it is dearness only that gives every thing its value.

Thomas Paine

There are some things you learn best in calm, and some in storm.

Willa Cather

Luck is an art.

George Roy Hill

Bad luck is only the superstitious excuse for those who don't have the wit to deal with the problems of life.

Joan Lowery Nixon

Nobody gets justice. People only get good luck or bad luck.

Orson Welles

Oh, I am fortune's fool!

William Shakespeare

One likes people much better when they're battered down by a prodigious siege of misfortune than when they triumph.

Virginia Woolf

Well done is better than well said.

Benjamin Franklin

Nature always wears the colours of the spirit.

Ralph Waldo Emerson

It is not how much we have, but how much we enjoy, that makes happiness.

Charles Spurgeon

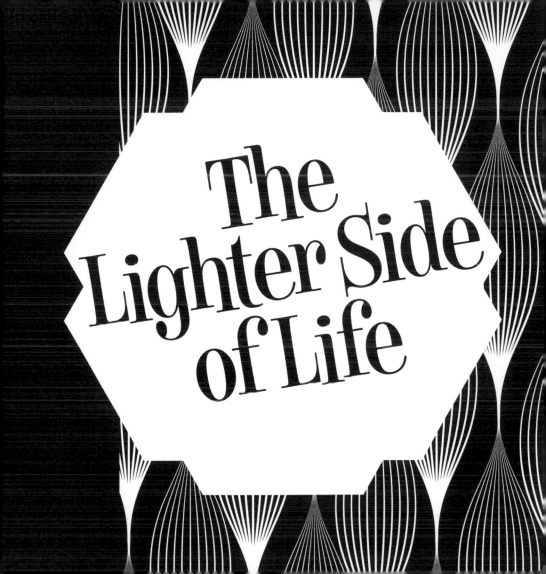

The Lighter Side of Life

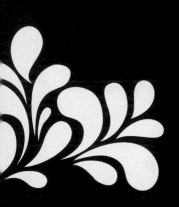

The difference between sex and love is that sex relieves tension and love causes it.

Woody Allen

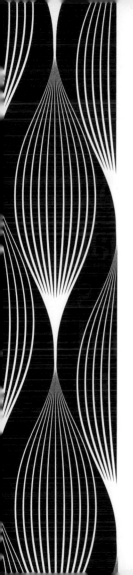

It is better of course to know useless things than to know nothing.

Seneca

A little inaccuracy sometimes saves a ton of explanation.

H.H. Munro

We get up by the clock, eat and sleep by the clock, get up again, go to work - and then we retire. And what do they give us? A clock.

Dave Allen

The pen is mightier than the sword, and considerably easier to write with.

Marty Feldman

A great many people think they are thinking when they are actually rearranging their prejudices.

William James

There's many a bestseller that could have been prevented by a good teacher.

Flannery O'Connor

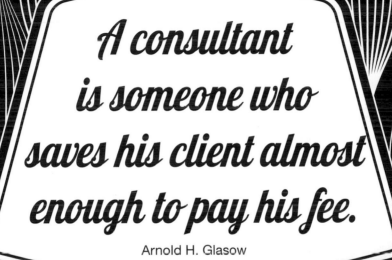

A consultant is someone who saves his client almost enough to pay his fee.

Arnold H. Glasow

Housework can't kill you, but why take a chance?

Phyllis Diller

It's not the voting that's democracy, it's the counting.

Tom Stoppard

It is dangerous to be right when the government is wrong.

Voltaire

I say if you love something, set it in a small cage and pester and smother it with love until it either loves you back or dies.

Mindy Kaling

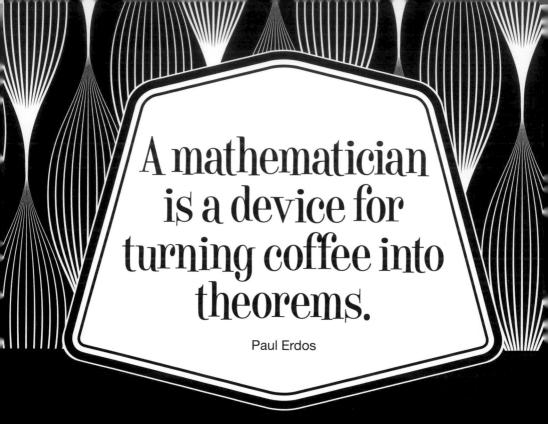

A mathematician is a device for turning coffee into theorems.

Paul Erdos

I am not young enough to know everything.

Oscar Wilde

I don't deserve this award, but I have arthritis and I don't deserve that either.

Jack Benny

They called me mad, and I called them mad, and damn them they out-voted me.

Nathaniel Lee

Sleep is an excellent way of listening to an opera.

James Stephens

An expert is a man who has made all the mistakes which can be made in a very narrow field.

Niels Bohr

Start every day off
with a smile and
get it over with.

W.C. Fields

The robbed
that smiles,
steals something
from the thief.

William Shakespeare

A mistake is simply another way of doing things.

Katharine Graham

Change generally pleases the rich.

Horace

The nice thing about being a celebrity is that if you bore people they think it's their fault.

Henry Kissinger

I can write better than anybody who can write faster, and I can write faster than anybody who can write better.

A.J. Liebling

Imitation is the sincerest form of television.

Fred Allen

Money couldn't buy friends, but you got a better class of enemy.

Spike Milligan

The man who smiles when things go wrong has thought of someone to blame it on.

Robert Bloch

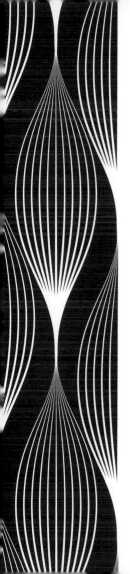

When choosing between two evils, I always like to try the one I've never tried before.

Mae West

It is a hard matter, my fellow citizens, to argue with the belly, since it has no ears.

Plutarch

I am free of all prejudice. I hate everyone equally.

W.C. Fields

Forgive your enemies,
but never forget their names.

John F. Kennedy

Decaffeinated coffee
is kind of like kissing
your sister.

Bob Irwin

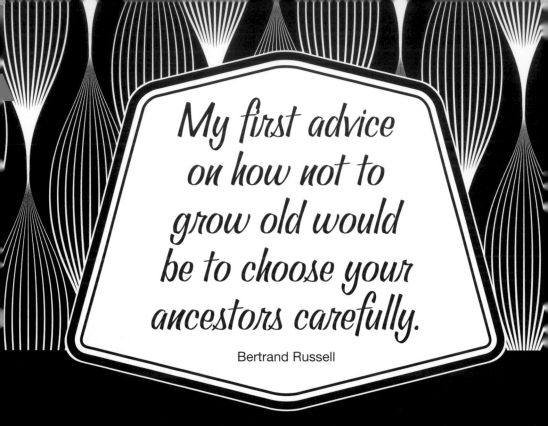

My first advice
on how not to
grow old would
be to choose your
ancestors carefully.

Bertrand Russell

I've had a wonderful time, but this wasn't it.

Groucho Marx

Watch out when you're getting all you want. Fattening hogs ain't in luck.

Joel Chandler Harris

Whenever you find yourself on the side of the majority, it is time to pause and reflect.

Mark Twain

I don't even butter my bread; I consider that cooking.

Katherine Cebrian

Whenever I feel the need to exercise, I lie down until it goes away.

Paul Terry

Human history becomes
more and more a race
between education
and catastrophe.

H.G. Wells

*My fake plants
died because I
did not pretend to
water them.*

Mitch Hedberg

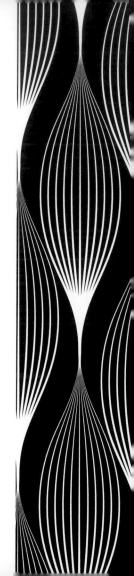

When a woman says, 'I have nothing to wear!', what she really means is, 'There's nothing here for who I'm supposed to be today'.

Caitlin Moran

She's the kind of girl who climbed the ladder of success wrong by wrong.

Mae West

Literature is mostly about having sex and not much about having children; life is the other way around.

David Lodge

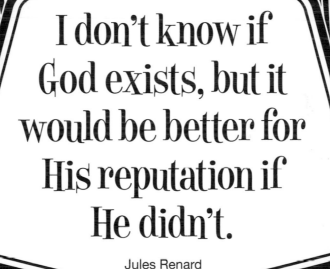

I don't know if God exists, but it would be better for His reputation if He didn't.

Jules Renard

Marriage is really tough because you have to deal with feelings and lawyers.

Richard Pryor

There is only one difference between a madman and me. I am not mad.

Salvador Dalí

My formula for success is rise early, work late, and strike oil.

Paul Getty

The power of accurate observation is frequently called cynicism by those who don't have it.

George Bernard Shaw

We are all atheists about most of the gods humanity has ever believed in. Some of us just go one god further.

Richard Dawkins

Conservatives are not necessarily stupid, but most stupid people are conservative.

John Stuart Mill

Everyone is a genius at least once a year; a real genius has his original ideas closer together.

Georg Lichtenberg

You know why divorces are so expensive? Because they're worth it.

Henny Youngman

Well-behaved women seldom make history.

Laurel Thatcher Ulrich

In the misfortune of our best friends we often find something that is not displeasing.

François de La Rouchefoucauld

No woman really wants a man to carry her off; she only wants him to want to do it.

Elizabeth Peters

A change of opinions is almost unknown in an elderly military man.

G.K. Chesterton

A humorist is a person who feels bad, but who feels good about it.

Don Herold

To be stupid, selfish, and have good health are three requirements for happiness, though if stupidity is lacking, all is lost.

Gustave Flaubert

Humans are the only animals that have children on purpose with the exception of guppies, who like to eat theirs.

P.J. O'Rourke

Love is the answer, but while you're waiting for the answer, sex raises some pretty good questions.

Woody Allen

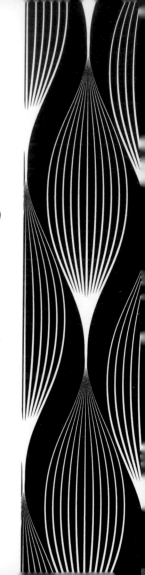

Before I met my husband,
I'd never fallen in love.
I'd stepped in it a few times.

Rita Rudner

Anything that is too stupid to be spoken is sung.

Voltaire

*A man's got
to do what a
man's got to do.
A woman must
do what he can't.*

Rhonda Hansome

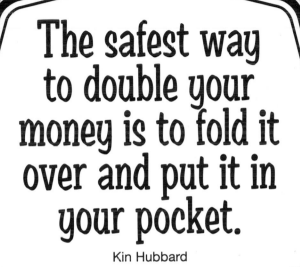

The safest way to double your money is to fold it over and put it in your pocket.

Kin Hubbard

A clever man commits no minor blunders.

Johann Wolfgang von Goethe

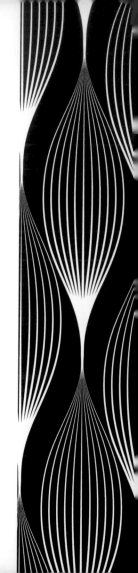

I'm a great housekeeper. I get divorced. I keep the house.

Zsa Zsa Gabor

The aim of
a joke is not
to degrade the
human being,
but to remind
him that he is
already degraded.

George Orwell

Analyzing humor is like dissecting a frog. Few people are interested and the frog dies of it.

E.B. White

Copy from one, it's plagiarism; copy from two, it's research.

Wilson Mizner

In three words I can sum up everything I've learned about life: it goes on.

Robert Frost

It is our responsibilities, not ourselves, that we should take seriously.

Peter Ustinov

A professor is someone who talks in someone else's sleep.

W.H. Auden

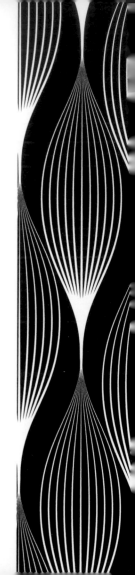

Tragedy is when I cut my finger. Comedy is when you walk into an open sewer and die.

Mel Brooks

My advice to you
is get married:
if you find a
good wife you'll
be happy;
if not, you'll
become a
philosopher.

Socrates

If you can't handle me at my worst, then you sure as hell don't deserve me at my best.

Marilyn Monroe

A man can't be too careful in the choice of his enemies.

Oscar Wilde

My best
birth control now
is just to leave
the lights on.

Joan Rivers

Love is grand; divorce is a hundred grand.

Shinichi Suzuki

I have never killed a man, but I have read many obituaries with great pleasure.

Clarence Darrow

Under democracy, one party always devotes its chief energies to trying to prove that the other party is unfit to rule - and both commonly succeed, and are right.

H.L. Mencken

Life is pleasant. Death is peaceful. It's the transition that's troublesome.

Isaac Asimov

I would like to be able to admire a man's opinions as I would his dog - without being expected to take it home with me.

Frank A. Clark

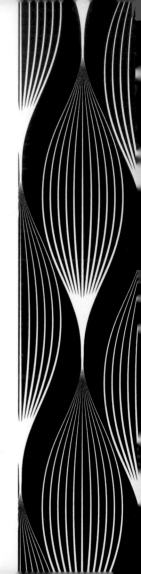

The worst part of success is to try to find someone who is happy for you.

Bette Midler

The best doctor is the one you run to and can't find.

Denis Diderot

I was married by a judge.
I should have asked for a jury.

Groucho Marx

I have never let my schooling interfere with my education.

Mark Twain

A wise woman puts
a grain of sugar in everything
she says to a man, and takes a grain
of salt with everything
he says to her.

Helen Rowland

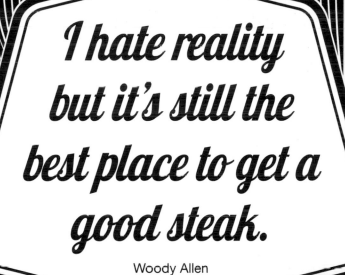

I hate reality but it's still the best place to get a good steak.

Woody Allen

Even the gods love jokes.

Plato

In 100 years we have gone from teaching Latin and Greek in high school to teaching Remedial English in college.

Joseph Sobran

When a man gives his opinion, he's a man. When a woman gives her opinion, she's a bitch.

Bette Davis

I am a great believer in luck. The harder I work, the more of it I seem to have.

Coleman Cox

A common mistake that people make when trying to design something completely foolproof is to underestimate the ingenuity of complete fools.

Douglas Adams

He was happily married - but his wife wasn't.

Victor Borge

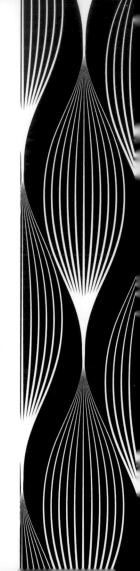

Sometimes I wonder if men and women really suit each other. Perhaps they should live next door and just visit now and then.

Katharine Hepburn

If you haven't got anything nice to say about anybody, come sit next to me.

Alice Roosevelt Longworth

Acting is all about honesty. If you can fake that, you've got it made.

George Burns